On the Political Podium

(A STAGE PLAY)

RUBABA MMAHAJIA RAHMA SABTIU

Rubaba Mmahajia Rahma Sabtiu

ON THE POLITICAL PODIUM (A STAGE PLAY)

CONTENT PAGE

ACKNOWLEDGEMENT

To all those who helped me in any way to make the writing and publishing of this play possible. I am extremely grateful...

Political Parties are like a team of players, each member with his or her personal agenda for being a part of the team even though the mission and vision ought to be the same. Some come for selfish motives yet there are those who come to better their people. To the former, a shame. To the latter, a praise...

Rubaba Mmahajia Rahma Sabtiu

DEDICATION

To the service of God Almighty

To my irreplaceable mum

To my family

To my friends

To Sheikh Sani Waleed

To my country Ghana for standing the test of political uproar

To the patriotic citizens of this country

To the Politician who has his/her country at heart

To you for reading it

'Loyalty to country ALWAYS.

Loyalty to government when it deserves it'

Mark Twain

INTRODUCTION

I thank God for the freedom of speech. There is a saying that; 'Opinions are like noses, everyone has one.' I like to put it as; 'Opinions are like flags, if you don't raise yours, no one sees it.' Talking about politics, I think flags fit it just fine. This is then my flag and I just raised it hoping that someone is going to see it.

I am not a political science student but rather an Agricultural (Agribusiness) student. Politics must be a concern of everyone because if it is clean or dirty, the impact is felt by everyone. Looking at Ghana, one realizes that even children are somehow involved in politics. The problem then is; how is our involvement in politics helping or not helping the development of our country? I am a citizen of Ghana, I have a freedom of speech and politics is a central point in the development of our country so I am concerned.

For me, politics is beyond important if the country is going to be taken care of as an entity. We cannot just live our lives just like that; waking up, doing business and going to sleep. Someone needs to be taking care of so many things for us all as we live our lives. That someone to me is the Politician because it is through politics that people get to become members of the government.

I will liken political parties to religion in the sense that there are various political parties and there are various religions. Each political party stands for something and it has followers who believe in it. Religion is also like that. The difference however is that; political parties unlike the various religions do not have the power to rule at all times. They gain power when they are elected to become the government. Religion shapes the moral of the people and politics give some people the mandate to define how the lives of everyone run every day.

Most people agree that politics is a game and it is a dirty one. The question that comes to my mind is; 'How dirty is politics?' and 'What do we even mean by 'Politics is a dirty game.' How I understand that is; 'One has to do all sorts of bad things to become a politician and then to become elected as government, politicians have to do a couple of very bad things as well. There is probably more to this dirty game thing than my little mind tells me.

There have been reports on cases where politicians have allegedly instigated some people to steal ballot boxes, vote multiple times, disregard votes for other political parties and many such. This is how far I can say politics is dirty to me. As to whether some politicians could go as far as killing people in order to get voted for, that is a whole new thing to me. And of course, some politicians make politics dirty by causing unnecessary political unrest among the people; the youth especially and also make corruption their business.

Rubaba Mmahajia Rahma Sabtiu

Another dirty aspect of politics is the fact that some politicians lie to protect their fame and also destroy the fame of their fellow politicians. They also make all sorts of sometimes impossible promises just to get votes from the innocent people.

So, there are very dirty things going on in politics that put all politicians in the spotlight. But the question is; 'Is it all politicians who are really making politics dirty?' 'What percentage of the politicians is involved in the dirty political game?' Most will say, 'the majority of them' but could they not be in the minority? Do we see how one rotten fish could make a whole bunch of them smell bad?

A team is made up of different categories of people with diverse backgrounds who come together to complement one another towards the achievement of a common goal. A team has got its strong points and its weak points. Some people could be an advantage to a team and some teams could be better off without some people.

A political party like a team is made up of different categories of people who complement one another towards achieving something for their country. At least, that should be the basic reason for political parties. It is funny however that some politicians probably don't have the country in mind as they do their politics.

One thing though that we cannot take out is the fact that there are politicians who are involved in politics because they want to make the situation of the country better. And I want to believe that for every political party, there are the bad ones and the good ones even if we cannot tell whether they have hidden agendas or not.

One thing for sure is that all the politicians do not have a common intention for being in politics. Some become politicians because it runs in the family; some because they got an opportunity along the way to join a political party, and some also enter politics deliberately. Some politicians have selfish motives for being in politics whilst others have very clean motives. There could be the politician who is involved in politics only because it makes him or her famous. Some also believe they could get a bigger share of the national cake by being politicians. And of course there are those who enter politics because they want to be a part of the nation's development and nothing else. Sometimes, some politicians make it obvious to the people their motives for being there whilst mostly one cannot tell.

A country will be better off if it has most of its 'political teams' made up of people who have the intention of making the country better off and not for mere fame and wealth. Will we be fair if we insult all politicians together with the ones with the good intentions? If yes, why should that be the case because we are supposed to be praying for more of these kinds of politicians? If no, how do we identify these types of politicians and exempt them from our insults?

Rubaba Mmahajia Rahma Sabtiu

When politicians decide to play their game by their own rules and they ignore the people they are supposed to be serving, then the people must do something; criticise. Criticism in the right way is a good thing and it serves as a check on the politicians who want to take the people for granted. This criticism should not be turned into insults because the politicians end up turning deaf ears on them. If we criticise politicians correctly, then they are forced to listen to us.

This book; 'On the Political Podium' 'A Stage Play' is my way of criticizing some dirty aspects of politics that are gradually eating into us. We could have people of different political parties living in peace at any point in time. It is however sad that most people consider their political opponents as their enemies. People insult, fight and even hurt one another for the sake of some politicians or the political parties they belong to.

The politicians who are mostly found hailing all sorts of accusations at one another and who also happen to be those who enjoy all the political powers, are seen after their political arguments having a good time with one another even though they belong to different political parties. Unfortunately, the followers of these political parties who do not benefit in the least from these political parties tend to create some enmity amongst themselves.

ON THE POLITICAL PODIUM (A STAGE PLAY)

People become so passionate about their political parties that they see everyone who does not belong to these parties as not being good enough. They treat one another with such an incredible contempt. It is also unfortunate that the literates who should know better are also found doing the same.

People have different reasons for belonging to different political parties. Some of the reasons are selfish and some are good. Every political party too has something good about it and something bad about it. For me, there is no one political party that is perfect. Belonging to different political parties is like belonging to different religions. Tolerating one another in such circumstances is the key to a peaceful co-existence. Our differences should not lead us to hate one another at all. We should cultivate the habit of tolerating and respecting one another's opinions and their decisions to belong to whichever political party they want. That is not also to say that we should not try to correct our political opponents when they are going wrong. That can be done by expressing our disagreement in a much nicer way. People have hot debates and arguments but they know that their everyday relationship should not be affected.

One thing that most politicians know how to do very well is to take the people for granted especially during election years. They would promise the people Paradise on earth just to get their votes. They promise the people things that they know themselves that they cannot provide. Some politicians use their campaign grounds as a lying platform both about their political opponents and to the people. They also make very feasible promises but which they don't end up doing when they are voted into power.

It is very sad however that most people fall for these kinds of deceit. One sure thing is that we would always have to make a choice among politicians and we cannot also have a perfect political team to lead us. It becomes a huge problem when all the political parties turn their campaign grounds into places for such things.

Politicians do not have to make promises that they cannot fulfil before they are voted for. They just have to be a little realistic with the people. They do not have to lie about one another just to win the favour of the people because that makes politics a very dirty game.

It is also very sad when the people make it binding upon themselves to vote for some political parties without considering how the party will be able to enhance the livelihood of the people and moving the country to another level of development. This play mimics such a situation of bad politics and the negative effects that come with it.

Enjoy every bit of it and take heed whilst you can.

RUBABA MMAHAJIA RAHMA SABTIU
29TH SEPTEMBER, 2013

ON THE POLITICAL PODIUM
(A poem)

In our ears

The sound of music

The singers sing on

From stages up high

Their voices echoing in our heads

The drummers drum on

A boost for the singers to sing on

Excitement fills the atmosphere

The dancers move to the rhythm

The rhythm that foretold the coming of a new day

A day full of hope

Hope for the end of despair

The despair that the people feel

Tears will be replaced by smiles

Yet to the child the drums' beats

And to the adult the singers' lyrics

By the Author

DISCLAIMER

All characters in this play are fictitious. Any resemblance to real persons, living or dead, is purely coincidental. I apologise if this play was unable to deliver the message in the most perfect manner to everyone. May God forgive me for any mistakes and accept my efforts. Please pray for all those who worked hard for this to become a reality. This play should not be staged without the prior permission of the author.

By the author

THE CAST

BAABA ADADA   An aged man with grey hair who walks with the aid of a walking stick.

BIG BEN   A vibrant young man who has been a vagabond most of his life

HASSANA   A young patriotic lady who is ready to give up her life for her country

YAW   A former accomplice and junior to Big Ben

ADAM   Another former accomplice and junior to Big Ben

KOFI   Also another accomplice and junior to Big Ben

ALHAJI YAHYA   A man who is trying to become the president of his country through dubious means

POLICE   A voice over

The seven deadly sins; wealth without work, pleasure without conscience, science without humanity, knowledge without character, politics without principle, commerce without morality and worship without sacrifice.

Mahatma Gandhi

Rubaba Mmahajia Rahma Sabtiu

PLAY BEGINS:

SCENE ONE:

IN BAABA ADADA'S HOUSE

(The sound of thunder is heard in the background and Baaba Adada's voice is heard)

BAABA ADADA:

(From the background) What a huge thunderstorm. Would the rain follow it? I love the dimness of the weather but I have to get home soon. Obviously, it is not going to rain but such weather is better enjoyed when at home *(He sings)*.

The deep blue sky is dazzling

Oh! See the white clouds too

And the birds are flying happily

I love the peace too

And I want to go home soon! *(He enters the stage looking exhausted)* Hmmm! I am running after old age too fast. Couldn't I hold time fixed so that I could swim in 2012 for at least five years before 2013? *(He laughs loudly)* That definitely wouldn't have been a bad idea. For now, I could spare a little nap before lunch. I have to follow the doctor's advice to survive *(Sound of dogs barking and cats meowing is heard in the background)*. The dogs are noisy and the cats too. Since when did the two fellows settle their long standing dispute? *(He lies on a mat with a pillow)* And what do they care about a poor old man trying to catch a peaceful nap? *(The barking of the dogs and meowing is replaced by the chirping of birds)* Now, that is what lulls one to sleep. Keep it up sweet birds of my town *(He begins to snore heavily as he lay on a mat and lights go out on stage and comes on again. Baaba Adada enters the stage looking much older and now walks with the aid of a walking stick. He soliloquys)* The elections are surely going to

16

be peaceful. Kwabena and Elorm believe that too. And something funny seems to be happening between those two of late! Does Elorm see a husband in Kwabena? *(He laughs loudly)* Me this old man, of course she does and this is surely not backbiting, is it? *(He sits down and picks a newspaper from a table)* And what does the newspaper say today? *(He overhears people talking in the background)*.

YAW:

(In the background) Do you believe we would win?

KOFI:

Of course! If we don't, nobody would!

BAABA ADADA:

(Shouting) Hey! Young men! What is wrong with you that you disturb the peace of an aged man? *(He stops as they continue talking)*.

YAW:

I am so afraid that something might go wrong. Do you think we would be paid if the party doesn't win?

KOFI:

Well, for me, losing is not an option after we made the youth register multiple times in order to vote massively for the party. And as for the party bosses, they better not play smart with us because we are the youth, we have all the strength *(Adam runs to them)*.

ADAM:

(Panting) Guys! Get ready! It looks like we have some problems coming up! Everything is indicating we might lose the election.

KOFI:

(Surprised) What? Incredible! After all that we are planning to do?

YAW:

(Sadly) I saw it coming. There could be trouble. Big trouble.

ADAM:

I've already informed everybody, all we need to do is act real fast and we can get things under control.

BAABA ADADA:

(Surprised) My God! Did I hear what I just heard! Young youthful men! You didn't say what you said, did you? *(He exits the stage and returns shortly)*

BAABA ADADA:

They are not there anymore. I have to stop them *(He is about to go out again but he stops)*. But no! Let me call the police first *(Something huge falls and an owl hoots)* What was that? An owl! An owl! Oh no! Not an owl! That is a bad omen. We cannot be in trouble. No, we cannot! And where is my phone? *(He removes a phone from his pocket and dials a number)* One, eight, five, five, five.

THE PHONE CALL

BAABA ADADA:

Hello! Is anyone there? *(A police responds in the background)*

POLICE:

Hi! Of course, there is someone here. What did you expect?

BAABA ADADA:

ON THE POLITICAL PODIUM (A STAGE PLAY)

And am I speaking with any of the police people?

POLICE:

Unbelievable! Didn't you dial the police hot line?

BAABA ADADA:

Yes, I did. But haven't you heard of fraudsters who can even forge your own being? And is that not what courtesy teach us? To ask who we are speaking to? Or did you have a fight with your wife today?

POLICE:

(Annoyed) Do you need our help or not?

BAABA ADADA:

(He laughs loudly) You are an African indeed. Why do you answer questions with questions?

POLICE:

Look here my friend, so many people need my service right now. It looks like you are not one of them.

BAABA ADADA:

Please wait! Don't hang up. I thought I needed help but I guess you also need some kind of help too.

POLICE:

(He heaves a sigh) I choose tolerance. How can I help you?

BAABA ADADA:

Rubaba Mmahajia Rahma Sabtiu

I would rather say; 'How can you help us?' You are the police so do something about those young men who are trying to cause trouble in our country.

POLICE:

Really! Who are those?

BAABA ADADA:

Let me finish. If you don't do something about them, you know you would surely lose your job and your wife would give you more trouble.

POLICE:

(Annoyed) Are you serious or you are joking?

BAABA ADADA:

(With seriousness) I never introduced myself to you as a clown. And note again, if your wife causes you more trouble, you would cause people like me who always vote for peace and tranquillity, a lot of distress.

POLICE:

(Angrily) I am going to lock you up very soon, Mister.

BAABA ADADA:

As to those seeking to cause trouble, they are three voices I heard a while ago. Their faces remain unknown to me so find them.

POLICE:

And how do you expect me to find them?

BAABA ADADA:

ON THE POLITICAL PODIUM (A STAGE PLAY)

Find them. You are the police and it is your duty to stop crime *(He ends the conversation)*.

BAABA ADADA:

I am setting out to fish for those boys. They need some counselling from the people of old *(He exits)*.

SCENE TWO:

A MEETING OF THE YOUTH

(Stage opens with Big Ben speaking to the audience)

BIG BEN:

(Talking passionately) The lions are wounded. The youth are troubled. If we lose this election, we lose all the promises we were made by the party bosses. We have been jobless. This is our opportunity to make easy money. Let us do anything we can to put our party bosses in power so that we can have a great share of the national cake.

SOUND FROM THE BACKGROUND: Yeah! Yeah! *(Hassana rushes inside)*

HASSANA:

(Angrily) Keep quiet! Pause and think! What are you saying to these innocent young men and women? Did you go to school when your parents forced you through? Did you not choose drugs over everything else you could have done?

BIG BEN:

(Provoked) Watch your words woman! You are stepping on my toes too hard.

HASSANA:

Brush it off! It is about time someone stands up to you and all those with you! *(There is an uproar in the background)*

BIG BEN:

Stay calm my people! Just stay calm and let me finish with her for good. Now, what is your problem with me?

ON THE POLITICAL PODIUM (A STAGE PLAY)

HASSANA:

Why would you let someone deceive you with a little amount of money to put the whole country into danger?

BIG BEN:

And what has the country given to me to deserve anything better?

HASSANA:

(She laughs loudly) Can you hear the echoes of your words? You register more than once and vote more than once.

BIG BEN:

(He ignores her) You don't have any sensible thing to say. *(To the audience)* My people, you know what to do, go ahead and do them with all your abilities. (He turns to Asana) The hunter in pursuit of an elephant does not stop to throw stones at birds *(He walks out on her)*.

HASSANA:

(She follows him) Where do you think you are going? Stand up to me if you can! *(She stops as Big Ben exits and turns to the audience)* My people! You have an option to do the right thing, don't listen to him *(Baaba Adada enters)*.

BAABA ADADA:

(Smiling) My pretty very young lady, can't you see all the people are gone?

HASSANA:

(Sadly) My respected elderly one, the people are trekking a wrong path.

BAABA ADADA:

Rubaba Mmahajia Rahma Sabtiu

Hmmm! Sadness and happiness reside in my heart at the same time my dear lady with youthful exuberance!

HASSANA:

Why is that respected one?

BAABA ADADA:

I feel sorrow for what I see and again I feel happy for what I see.

HASSANA:

(Confused) You are not speaking clearly respected one.

BAABA ADADA:

Young men and women whose strength could bring great development to us have rather turned against the country. They drag it straight into destruction.

HASSANA:

(Her eyes are teary) That definitely makes you sad. It makes me sad as well. And for me, I see no joy in the day. What could be making you happy?

BAABA ADADA:

This is why I am happy *(He begins to recite).*

Looking back to those days

The days when I was a little boy

Men gave commands

Women obeyed

ON THE POLITICAL PODIUM (A STAGE PLAY)

Men spoke all the time

Women kept mute

How dare her utter a word

How dare her challenge the man when he spoke

Even when he was obviously wrong

HASSANA:

(Smiling) This is a beautiful poetry.

BAABA ADADA:

(He continues)

Whether she is happy

Whether she is sad

That was not important *(He pauses)*

HASSANA:

Those indeed were hard times for us. Are you a poet?

BAABA ADADA:

(He continues reciting)

Hard times she had

Her tears never flowed on her cheeks

It went back straight to her heart

Where no one cared to wipe it off

Rubaba Mmahajia Rahma Sabtiu

Today I see something nice

A young lady challenges a young man

She tells him in the face

You are wrong! You are wrong!

She fears no one and her tears freely flows

One does not need to be a poet to describe this woman *(He stops)*

HASSANA:

(She laughs happily as she rubs off the tears with her hand) My tears!

BAABA ADADA:

Clean your tears young lady. Your strength has been made clear from your weakness. We need more of you in the system.

HASSANA:

Thank you for appreciating my efforts. Sometimes all that one can do is to speak out her sorrow.

BAABA ADADA:

Let us go and stand tall for our motherland *(They exit).*

SCENE THREE:

RTP RALLY GROUNDS

(Stage opens with Alhaji Yahya and Big Ben talking to the audience as Yaw, Kofi, Adam, Hassana and Baaba Adada looked on)

YAW, KOFI AND ADAM:

(Shouting energetically) RTP! RTP! RTP!

ALHAJI YAHYA:

Oh you loyal members of Reformation Today Party! You make me happy and proud! Vote for me! Vote for me! Vote for me! Vote for me because I ought to be president! Vote for me for I ought to be president!

BIG BEN:

Vote for him! Vote for him! Vote for him because we need him to be president!

YAW, KOFI AND ADAM:

RTP! RTP! RTP!

ALHAJI YAHYA:

I promise you everything that you can dream about. What do you want? Beautiful houses and cars? The latest phones? The latest clothes? Do you want to travel abroad? I, Alhaji Yahya, the president to be, promises you all that. Just vote for me! Vote for me! I ought to be your president!

BIG BEN:

Rubaba Mmahajia Rahma Sabtiu

Our leaders have failed us badly. We are arrested and sent to prison for trivial issues. We are jobless. We do not have good shelter! We are deprived of the things that make our life comfortable. Vote for Alhaji! Vote for him! He understands our dreams better!

ALHAJI YAHYA:

Oh yes! I do.

BIG BEN:

He wouldn't drive us out of our ghettos.

ALHAJI YAHYA:

No, I wouldn't. I will make them better.

BIG BEN:

RTP! RTP!

YAW, KOFI AND ADAM:

RTP! RTP! RTP!

BIG BEN:

He promises to bring to us our brothers and sisters who are rotting in our prisons.

ALHAJI YAHYA:

I promise to release all of them and make life as easy for you as possible. Just vote for me. I ought to be president *(The sound of Big Ben and Alhaji Yahya's voice fade as they continue talking)*.

HASSANA:

ON THE POLITICAL PODIUM (A STAGE PLAY)

(Surprised) Unbelievable indeed. What kind of vain promises are those?

YAW:

(Provoked) Who told you they are vain promises?

HASSANA:

And who are you?

YAW:

(Proudly) A loyal member of RTP.

HASSANA:

(Sarcastically) And are you proud to be a member of this unrealistic party?

YAW:

How do you mean? *(Baaba Adada stares at Yaw)*

BAABA ADADA:

(Trying to recall something) Hmmm! Your voice rings a bell.

YAW:

(Angry) I have never seen you before old man.

BAABA ADADA:

Take it easy young man. Neither have I. I said your voice.

YAW:

All right. It looks like you two are not interested in the promises. I want to pay attention to what Alhaji has for us. It is important to me. So, if you will excuse me *(He moves away from them)*.

Rubaba Mmahajia Rahma Sabtiu

HASSANA:

No wait!

BAABA ADADA:

Let him go. You cannot talk any sense into him in such an environment that is so full of deceit.

HASSANA:

Respected one.

BAABA ADADA:

Yes, my youthful young lady.

HASSANA:

(Boldly) Please give me permission to go and interrogate Alhaji Yahya in front of the people.

BAABA ADADA:

(Clapping and smiling) You indeed are a brave woman!

HASSANA:

Do I have permission?

BAABA ADADA:

I have lived so many years in this life young lady. My grey hair tells that better. Asking for permission to do something like that is like asking for permission to go and get killed. One does not use her bare feet to search for hidden thorns which she has seen in day time my daughter.

ON THE POLITICAL PODIUM (A STAGE PLAY)

HASSANA:

(Bravely) No! No! No! They cannot kill me! They can never kill me! It is God who causes death and if He doesn't cause my death, no one can!

BAABA ADADA:

(He laughs) I agree with you my lady. The problem is that God's time for your death might just coincide with their timing for your death sweet lady.

HASSANA:

How do you mean respected one?

BAABA ADADA:

To the stupid child, one speaks in very plain language but to the wise one, one speaks in proverbs.

HASSANA:

(Confused) I still don't understand you wise one.

BAABA ADADA:

Tonight when you sleep, ask your pillow, it has all the answers to all the questions you have.

HASSANA:

So...

BAABA ADADA:

So, you don't have permission for suicide. Let's go and find another way of doing the same thing.

Rubaba Mmahajia Rahma Sabtiu

HASSANA:

(Reluctant) But… well, if you say so.

BAABA ADADA:

Wait! It looks like they are about to wrap up *(Alhaji Yahya and Big Ben's voices are heard)*

ALHAJI YAHYA:

Vote for me! Vote for me! Vote for me for I ought to be president!

BIG BEN:

RTP! RTP! RTP! Vote for him! For he ought to be president! *(Alhaji Yahya and Big Ben begin to move away)*

HASSANA:

They are dispersing so we can go now *(Yaw starts moving out with Kofi and Adam)*.

BAABA ADADA:

(Pointing at Yaw and his friends) Look at the young man you were trying to convince. He has two companions with him.

HASSANA:

Why are they going a separate way from Alhaji Yahya and Big Ben?

BAABA ADADA:

Don't you have something to catch up with him for?

HASSANA:

What? Oh! Yes, I do *(She walks quickly towards Yaw and his friends)* Mister! Mister! Mister!

ON THE POLITICAL PODIUM (A STAGE PLAY)

ADAM:

(He turns to look at her) Me?

HASSANA:

(Panting) No, him *(She points to Yaw)*

YAW:

(Yaw turns to look at her) This lady again. What do you want this time around?

HASSANA:

Forgive me if I am interfering but could you give me a few minutes of your time?

YAW:

(He laughs) You do have some guts, don't you? And you expect me to give you that?

ADAM:

Just go and listen to what she has to say and let us go. We do not have time to waste.

HASSANA:

(She smiles at Adam) Thank you very much *(She moves aside with Yaw and then she takes a pen and a small sheet of paper from her pocket. She begins to write)*

YAW:

(Surprised) What are you writing?

HASSANA:

(She hands the paper to him) Please take this piece of paper. All that I want to talk to you about is on it. Don't let anyone see it *(She walks quickly back to Baaba Adada).*

Rubaba Mmahajia Rahma Sabtiu

YAW:

Hey! Hey! What is the meaning of this?

KOFI:

Let's go if you are done with her *(Yaw put the paper in his pocket and the three of them exit)*.

HASSANA:

(Happily) I hope he obeys, respected one.

BAABA ADADA:

Let us hope for the best. I am proud of you young lady.

HASSANA:

I am glad respected one. I have learnt a lot from you today *(They exit)*.

ON THE POLITICAL PODIUM (A STAGE PLAY)

SCENE FOUR:

IN BAABA ADADA'S HOUSE

BAABA ADADA:

Today I hear no sound of rain. The clouds aren't so attractive either. Sad is their gaze upon the soil. A few moments ago, I wanted to prolong 2013 for as long as possible. Now, is 2013 not gone already? Today has been a year full of mixed feelings. I am very stressed up and I need nothing but rest. (*Dogs barking and cats meowing*) They have started again. They never want to give an old man a quiet time. But don't they have the right to bark and meow as much as they want? Who am I to deprive them of their God-given rights? (*He hears voices in the background*).

ADAM:

You seem extra quiet, Yaw?

YAW:

Really?

KOFI:

Yes, that is true. Is there any problem?

YAW:

No, not at all.

KOFI:

(*Laughing*) Or is it about that pretty lady who was on your neck earlier?

ADAM:

(*He feigns a cough*) Oho! I get it now. Is she your new catch? She isn't bad at all (*Kofi and Adam laugh at Yaw teasingly*) Isn't this interesting? Yaw of all people feeling down because of a girl.

Rubaba Mmahajia Rahma Sabtiu

BAABA ADADA:

(He laughs happily) Young men of today, all they think about are women. Have they not heard that women were the woes of men? *(He laughs loudly)* But wait! Those voices are very familiar.

YAW:

(Calmly) That young lady argued with me about Alhaji Yahya's promises. She said they were vain.

BAABA ADADA:

(Surprised) My God! It is that young man Hassana spoke to *(He goes to stand close to the exit and peeps outside)* I wish I could see them a little clearer.

KOFI:

(Annoyed) Brush it off, Yaw. That young lady doesn't know what she is talking about. I actually thought it was something important that was bothering your mind.

ADAM:

(Also annoyed) Me too. How do you believe this little girl who is ignorant about what is going on? And please, don't be a coward. I have never known you to be one.

YAW:

I wouldn't agree with you much. I have always had my fears. Caution is not cowardice for even the ants march armed. Besides, that so called little girl sounds very intelligent. You should speak to her to verify.

ADAM:

We are the youth. We have all the strength. That old Alhaji Yahya cannot play with us. Besides Big Ben has everything under control.

ON THE POLITICAL PODIUM (A STAGE PLAY)

BAABA ADADA:

I can see them now. It is those same three gentlemen at the campaign grounds.

YAW:

You know what? Let me go and check on something at home. I will see you later.

ADAM:

But don't we have a lot to do right now?

KOFI:

Let's go. He is gone already. We will talk about it when he returns.

BAABA ADADA:

My God! These were the voices that I heard this morning. *(Smiling)* I finally caught them *(He pauses)*. And could the young man be going to meet Hassana as planned? If yes, could she handle him? Well, that young lady has energy and a good sense to stand anyone *(He pauses)*. Or should I call the police to arrest them? *(He laughs loudly)* That man is so full of humour that I would love to talk to him once again *(He pauses)*. Oh no! That is not a good idea at all. They would surely ask for evidence and I don't have any. I guess I need to find evidence first *(He exits)*.

SCENE FIVE:

HASSANA AND YAW MEET

(Hassana enters and starts pacing the stage)

HASSANA:

(Worried) It looks like this man will never come. What even made me think of such a weird idea? *(She pauses to think)* But Baaba Adada is an old wise man who knows what he says.

YAW:

(Entering from behind her) So, that old man told you to summon me here!

HASSANA:

(She turns in excitement) You are here.

YAW:

Yes, I am here. Now start.

HASSANA:

Start what?

YAW:

You called me for a reason, didn't you?

HASSANA:

Yes, I did.

YAW:

ON THE POLITICAL PODIUM (A STAGE PLAY)

Proceed then. Time and tide wait for no man.

HASSANA:

But you should know why I called you here, shouldn't you?

YAW:

You wanted to propose…

HASSANA:

(Defensive) Oh please! Propose to you for what?

YAW:

(Surprised) This is interesting indeed. What are you thinking?

HASSANA:

Nothing!

YAW:

And I actually believed you were such a brave lady.

HASSANA:

I surely am but I don't do those kinds of things.

YAW:

And what are those things if I may ask?

HASSANA:

I don't propose to men.

YAW:

I never said you do *(He pauses and laughs)*. I get it. You got me all wrong young lady.

HASSANA:

How do you mean?

YAW:

All right, listen to me very carefully. I didn't mean that you wanted to propose to me like a woman would propose to a man for them to be in a sexual relationship. I meant that you wanted to present a proposal, a political proposal, to me. At least, that was what I read from the note you gave me at the campaign grounds.

HASSANA:

(Laughing) How very silly of me. I am sorry for misunderstanding you. Those words are troublesome indeed.

YAW:

So then can we proceed because there is so much I can do right now to make sure that Alhaji Yahya gets addressed as His Excellency, the President?

HASSANA:

I do not have any problems with you helping in his campaign but I have a problem with your inability to decipher his deceitful means of campaigning.

YAW:

And why do you insist that his promises are vain?

HASSANA:

Because his promises are vain.

ON THE POLITICAL PODIUM (A STAGE PLAY)

YAW:

Don't you know that a president has the right to do just about everything he wants?

HASSANA:

That is not true.

YAW:

Is that not what all the presidents that we have known do?

HASSANA:

That is not also true.

YAW:

See young lady, for me, all that is important is that he becomes the president so that he could do something essential for me and my friends especially.

HASSANA:

That is very interesting.

YAW:

The truth however is that I have always entertained some kind of fear about Alhaji Yahya. I don't really trust him.

HASSANA:

Oh! I see.

YAW:

So, what would you say about Mr Kotei Mawuli?

Rubaba Mmahajia Rahma Sabtiu

HASSANA:

What about him?

YAW:

Do you think his promises are real?

HASSANA:

(She laughs loudly) Is he not even worse?

YAW:

You seem like a very impossible person.

HASSANA:

If it is in this context, then that would be a perfect description of me.

YAW:

But at least his promises are not cars, houses and phones. He promises better things.

HASSANA:

Better things like easy access to visas to countries that you have nothing doing in?

YAW:

And what makes you think that if I am given the opportunity to go to America, I wouldn't make it big?

HASSANA:

Because even in your own country, you are not doing anything to make your standard of living better.

ON THE POLITICAL PODIUM (A STAGE PLAY)

YAW:

See, I would like to talk to you some more but I would have to go now. Let's meet at this same place again tomorrow. There are a lot of things I want us to talk about.

HASSANA:

That is not a problem at all. Thank you for your time.

YAW:

You are welcome *(They exit in different directions)*.

SCENE SIX:

IN BAABA ADADA'S HOUSE

(Baaba Adada enters and he begins to sing)

BAABA ADADA:

We are going.

Heaven knows where we are going.

We will get there *(He ends and comes to sit).*

Hassana has kept too long. Is it that she is not done with him already? Could it also be that she couldn't get the direction to my house well? There are too many questions but no answers *(He hears an owl hooting).* My God! An owl again? This is a bad omen. What has happened to Hassana? Did I push her into the hands of wicked men? What have they done to her? What do I do? *(He paused)* But she has a home; she could probably have gone to her home. I don't need to worry. *(He paused again)* But no! I have to call the police. *(He takes a phone out of his pocket and dials)* One, eight, five, five, five.

THE SECOND PHONE CALL

BAABA ADADA:

Hello! Is anyone there?

POLICE:

(Talking from the background) Hi! Somebody is definitely here.

BAABA ADADA:

Am I speaking to the police?

ON THE POLITICAL PODIUM (A STAGE PLAY)

POLICE:

Who else do you expect to be speaking to?

BAABA ADADA:

(He laughs) So it is my old friend on the line again.

POLICE:

Who is this?

BAABA ADADA:

It is I, Baaba Adada.

POLICE:

And how many Baaba Adadas are there in this country?

BAABA ADADA:

Only one. Only one.

POLICE:

I see. And you expect me to know you? Are you a celebrity or something?

BAABA ADADA:

(He laughs) That will depend on your definition of a celebrity. The last time I checked, no one celebrates me.

POLICE:

(He begins to laugh too) I think I know who I am talking to now.

BAABA ADADA:

Rubaba Mmahajia Rahma Sabtiu

Aha! Now, you are being as smart as you should be. You were hired for that purpose. Always remember that.

POLICE:

(Excited) It is the funny old voice again.

BAABA ADADA:

Old voice? My body may be old but my voice is like that of a young lad *(They both laugh)*. So how is your wife treating you now?

POLICE:

She is treating me like a king. Have you had any information on those voices you wanted us to arrest?

BAABA ADADA:

I have seen the faces of those voices.

POLICE:

That is good news. Give me their details.

BAABA ADADA:

I do not have details. I could take their pictures later but I don't have any evidence against them for now.

POLICE:

(Annoyed) What is the use of your call then?

ON THE POLITICAL PODIUM (A STAGE PLAY)

BAABA ADADA:

The use of my call is that you now know those voices have faces so go and search for them before you bite your nails. And I also made you laugh *(He hangs up).* Sometimes one shouldn't talk too much to convey a simple message *(He stands up, starts pacing the stage and exits).*

SCENE SEVEN:

YAW AND KOFI MEET

(Stage opens with Kofi sitting alone in a corner. Yaw enters)

YAW:

Why are you alone, Kofi? Where is Adam?

KOFI:

(Turning to Yaw) You two left me alone.

YAW:

Where did Adam say he was going?

KOFI:

Where else other than the usual place.

YAW:

So are we not going for the meeting anymore?

KOFI:

It has been adjourned to tomorrow.

YAW:

(Surprised) What! A day before the election?

KOFI:

Yes. And why do you sound so surprised?

ON THE POLITICAL PODIUM (A STAGE PLAY)

YAW:

Don't you think it is a bit risky?

KOFI:

Is it riskier than all the things we have done before in our lives?

YAW:

Well…

KOFI:

Don't let that girl deceive you with her philosophies. The temptations of women are slippery. One easily falls into it.

YAW:

Forget about that girl. Could you brief me on some of the basic things we are required to do? I missed the meeting earlier.

KOFI:

It is simple. Just try as much as you can to vote more than once at different polling stations for Alhaji Yahya and assist others to do the same.

YAW:

(Smiling) That is quiet easy but I heard TCP also has the same plan. What if they succeed in having the highest votes?

KOFI:

We will steal some of the ballot boxes at areas where they have strong points of winning.

Rubaba Mmahajia Rahma Sabtiu

YAW:

Well, I hope that works out well. We have to get going then *(They exit).*

ON THE POLITICAL PODIUM (A STAGE PLAY)

SCENE EIGHT:

IN BAABA ADADA'S HOUSE

(Baaba Adada sits quietly. There is a knock on the door)

BAABA ADADA:

Who is it please?

HASSANA:

It is I, Hassana.

BAABA ADADA:

Oh! Hassana. You may come inside *(She enters)*. I thought something bad had happened to you.

HASSANA:

I am very fine wise one.

BAABA ADADA:

Please come and have a seat my young lady *(He points to a chair and she comes to sit)*.

HASSANA:

Thank you. Good evening Baaba.

BAABA ADADA:

Good evening my dear daughter.

BAABA ADADA:

(Smiling) Strong women always return safely. You are welcome strong woman.

Rubaba Mmahajia Rahma Sabtiu

HASSANA:

Thank you Baaba.

BAABA ADADA:

I had three sons with no daughter. If I had a daughter, I would have wanted her to be just like you.

HASSANA:

(Blushing) Thank you Baaba. Where are your family?

BAABA ADADA:

Before I answer that, what may I offer you? *(He stands up)*

HASSANA:

Nothing, Baaba. I am ok.

BAABA ADADA:

No, my dear young lady. It is courtesy to take something when you pay someone a visit. At least water would be good for you.

HASSANA:

Ok then wise one.

BAABA ADADA:

Do you want it chilled or as I want it, natural?

HASSANA:

Chilled.

ON THE POLITICAL PODIUM (A STAGE PLAY)

BAABA ADADA:

Ok *(He exits and comes back with a glass of chilled water on a tray)*. Here you are *(He sits)*.

HASSANA:

Thank you wise one *(She drinks it all)*. It feels very refreshing.

BAABA ADADA:

Should I get you some more?

HASSANA:

No, Baaba, it is all right *(She puts the tray on a nearby table)*.

BAABA ADADA:

You drank it all, meaning, you really needed it.

HASSANA:

Yes, I did but I am very ok now. Thank you.

BAABA ADADA:

So, how did your meeting go?

HASSANA:

It was all right just that he was very argumentative.

BAABA ADADA:

That is expected.

HASSANA:

And we didn't reach any compromise.

BAABA ADADA:

Really? How did it end?

HASSANA:

He said we should meet again tomorrow.

BAABA ADADA:

(Surprised) A day before the election?

HASSANA:

Yes. A day before the election.

BAABA ADADA:

Well, we have to be a little careful with him then. And do you think he would buy into your idea of peace?

HASSANA:

I cannot tell Baaba. He looks very unpredictable.

BAABA ADADA:

Let us hope for the best then. In life, one has to just keep trying.

HASSANA:

But Baaba, you haven't told me about your family.

BAABA ADADA:

I need to know about your family as well.

ON THE POLITICAL PODIUM (A STAGE PLAY)

HASSANA:

I was the first to ask.

BAABA ADADA:

Look at the time.

HASSANA:

(She looks at her wrist watch and she stands up in surprise) My God! It is almost 6 pm.

BAABA ADADA:

Your family would be worried so you have to go home.

HASSANA:

Yes, I have to. My parents are going to be very angry.

BAABA ADADA:

Tell them that you were on a national assignment.

HASSANA:

They don't care about national assignments.

BAABA ADADA:

(Jokingly) Then tell them to fold their hands and wait for trouble to engulf them.

HASSANA:

I wish I could make them see the impact of their I-don't-care attitude.

BAABA ADADA:

Try your best. And always remember that, you can only try and hope for the best.

Rubaba Mmahajia Rahma Sabtiu

HASSANA:

Ok. Good bye Baaba. I will see you tomorrow God willing.

BAABA ADADA:

Good bye. My regards to your family *(She exits)*. See how blessed Hassana's parents are yet they fail to see the jewel they possess. Hmmm! If only they knew. Let me go and put two and two together. There is so much to be done to ensure peace in this country. May God help us *(He stands up and exits)*

ON THE POLITICAL PODIUM (A STAGE PLAY)

SCENE NINE:

(Big Ben enters with vigour)

BIG BEN:

(He starts pacing the stage) Tomorrow, we go to the polls. It is a must win for RTP. No other party would rule this country except RTP. If they win, we will not make them rule *(Hassana enters from an opposite direction)*.

HASSANA:

(Surprised to see him) It seems that we are always crossing each other's path.

BIG BEN:

(He points to her) You! I have seen your face somewhere before.

HASSANA:

(Smiling) It is quite interesting that you don't remember exactly where you had an encounter with me.

BIG BEN:

(Nodding his head) I remember *(He laughs loudly)*. The woman who dared to stand up against me.

HASSANA:

I particularly love the fact that you remember that I stood up against you.

BIG BEN:

You wouldn't be doing the same from tomorrow onwards. That is a promise.

HASSANA:

Rubaba Mmahajia Rahma Sabtiu

And why is that if I may ask?

BIG BEN:

Because we are going to win the elections come what may and people like you will be taught hard lessons. Very hard lessons.

HASSANA:

(She laughs loudly) Aren't you interesting? And by 'we' who and who do you mean?

BIG BEN:

(Provoked) And you even have the audacity to laugh at me? You will regret this much sooner than you think. I am warning you!

HASSANA:

Stay calm. May I know how come you are so sure of winning?

BIG BEN:

Because we are going to win and as to how we are going to do that it is none of your business.

HASSANA:

Through all the dubious means you can lay your hands on, I guess. What else could it possibly be?

BIG BEN:

If you know, why do you ask Madam Holier-Than-Thou?

ON THE POLITICAL PODIUM (A STAGE PLAY)

HASSANA:

I keep wondering. Do you know what the four other political parties are doing in order to win this election?

BIG BEN:

I have information on all of their plans. We will surely outwit them.

HASSANA:

And why would you allow them to take you all for a free ride like that?

BIG BEN:

If I may ask, which party do you belong to?

HASSANA:

I can't see myself belonging to deceit in the name of political parties provided they would put you through all these just to win an election.

BIG BEN:

(Surprised) So, to you all political parties are corrupt?

HASSANA:

No! Don't get me wrong. To me, all political parties should have principles that will make them do their campaigns genuinely and use genuine means to get into power other than what I am seeing.

BIG BEN:

Ok, Madam Principles. You have to know however that at the end of the day, we have to choose one of these political parties to see to the affairs of this country so why are you bothering yourself? Or do you intend to form your own political party?

Rubaba Mmahajia Rahma Sabtiu

HASSANA:

(Calmly) No, I don't.

BIG BEN:

(Laughing) So then you see my dear lady, we have no choice. We have to take advantage of the opportunities that come our way to make life better for ourselves. Opportunity comes once, remember?

HASSANA:

(She turns to the audience and speak sadly) As the brave cry, the cowards laugh. Do they have any idea what it means to set ablaze their own shelter? *(She turns to Big Ben)* No, we do have a choice. We definitely have a choice.

BIG BEN:

Talk to me about the choices we have then and do so quickly because I have no time to waste.

HASSANA:

(Reciting)

We are the youth

We have the strength

Why do we watch them lie to us?

Must they become powerful?

Just for them to forget us later?

Must we always be the tool?

ON THE POLITICAL PODIUM (A STAGE PLAY)

For our own destruction?

BIG BEN:

(Angry) Stop woman! What are you insinuating?

HASSANA:

(She continues)

In our ghettos they come

From their plush houses

Riding in posh cars

Telling us to play all the dirty games

Promising us lies

We the youth

We those with the strength

Must we succumb to deceit? *(She stops)*

BIG BEN:

(Calmly) Hmmm! I… I… Forget it.

HASSANA:

Did you understand me, Big Ben?

BIG BEN:

(Surprised) You know my name?

Rubaba Mmahajia Rahma Sabtiu

HASSANA:

Who doesn't know your name? Did you understand me? *(He does not respond).* Besides, you are not getting my point at all. I know very well that somebody has to take over the affairs of this country but then you and I should know that we should help them to do so in the best manner. The political parties are a team. Some have bad intentions and others have good intentions. We cannot know who is good and who is bad except by looking at what each one of them does. If someone will let you do these nasty things just so he could become powerful, wouldn't you advise yourself about that person? *(Big Ben stares at her quietly)* Now, that is what I am talking about. Do you understand? *(Baaba Adada enters).*

BAABA ADADA:

(Smiling) By his facial expression, I am more than sure that he has understood your every word.

BIG BEN:

(Surprised) You this old man! *(He begins to laugh)* So it is you who is called the wise one and you are teaching her *(He points to Hassana)* all that. *(Sarcastically)* Don't you think that your old age is probably disturbing your thinking abilities? *(He laughs loudly).*

HASSANA:

(Angrily) Big Ben! Show some respect. *(She turns to Baaba Adada)* You are welcome respected one.

BAABA ADADA:

(He smiles) Thank you my dear Hassana. I hope you are doing well.

HASSANA:

Yes, I am by God's grace.

ON THE POLITICAL PODIUM (A STAGE PLAY)

BAABA ADADA:

(He turns to Big Ben) You see, there is a lot of wisdom in why the child is forewarned about laughing at the ugliness of her mother. If she were to keep a photo of herself, in a couple of years, she will find out the answer to why she was pre-warned. But Big Ben, you didn't respond to Hassana's question.

BIG BEN:

Sorry but I have to go. *(To the audience)* When all men say you are a dog, then know that it is time for you to start barking *(He begins to walk away)*.

HASSANA:

So, you are not shy to run away.

BIG BEN:

(Angrily) Don't you dare annoy me!

BAABA ADADA:

(He moves closer to Big Ben) Pardon her Big Ben.

BIG BEN:

Why does she speak as if she knows everything?

BAABA ADADA:

Please pardon her.

HASSANA:

I am sorry if I offended you.

Rubaba Mmahajia Rahma Sabtiu

BIG BEN:

(Devastated) You two have had life easy so you can talk about peace or whatever. What has the country done for me in order for me to give it anything better? If you breed up a serpent, he strikes when you are in deep slumber. The country is only reaping what it has sowed in me.

BAABA ADADA:

Big Ben, I believe the country does a lot for you to deserve something good from you. You probably haven't thought about it.

BIG BEN:

I have lived in hardship all my life. My parents never bothered to take care of me. I have lived in ghettos. I have eaten from the rubbish dump. I have worn tattered clothes. What contribution has the country made in my life?

BAABA ADADA:

I'm sorry for the hardship you had to go through.

BIG BEN:

And you think feeling sorry for me is enough to make up for all the bad times I have had?

HASSANA:

Do you have to blame the country and its inhabitants for the troubles that you had to endure?

BIG BEN:

I never said I blamed the country. I said I haven't had any reason not to campaign for the one I believe could give me what I never had all my life in this country.

ON THE POLITICAL PODIUM (A STAGE PLAY)

HASSANA:

And that is the more reason why we are trying to make you see the reality of the fact that Alhaji Yahya and all the others who make you do the bad jobs so that they could win are just lying to you.

BAABA ADADA:

They are making use of the fact that you have had a bad life to make you promises they can never fulfil and they will not fulfil even if they could.

BIG BEN:

I am not the only one involved.

BAABA ADADA:

Are all the others not from the ghettos as well? Why would they go to those places where they believe criminals mostly reside to instigate you people to do the very crimes they put you in prison for?

BIG BEN:

And what is the difference between what awaits me if I help Alhaji Yahya and if I don't?

BAABA ADADA:

At least you would still have your country to live in peacefully.

HASSANA:

A place to call your own.

BAABA ADADA:

And that is the most important thing if you but knew.

Rubaba Mmahajia Rahma Sabtiu

BIG BEN:

(Crying) You probably don't understand.

BAABA ADADA:

And you probably don't understand what it means to have a peaceful country to live in, do you?

BIG BEN:

For the few months I have come to know Alhaji Yahya, my life is a thousand times better else you wouldn't be so comfortable speaking with me like you are doing now.

BAABA ADADA:

(Smiling to the audience) It is only the fool who judges people by the presents they give him. *(To Big Ben)* I wouldn't use the word better if I were you.

HASSANA:

And hasn't the criminal things you do increased?

BIG BEN:

And am I the only one doing the so called criminal things?

HASSANA:

If you stop and convince another person to stop, we will be heading towards something positive.

BIG BEN:

(Frustrated) And really, I repeat, what has the country done for me to deserve anything better?

HASSANA: *(Angrily)* Because the country gave you a home and even the mightiest eagle comes down to the tree tops to rest after a hard day in the skies. Home is home.

ON THE POLITICAL PODIUM (A STAGE PLAY)

BAABA ADADA:

(Sorrowfully)

A grey hair and wrinkled skin are not easy to come by

There are reasons why a strong man suddenly goes weak

Walking with difficulty he who used to be the strongest

HASSANA:

Baaba, you sound sorrowful.

BIG BEN:

Hmmm! Can't you see sorrow on his face?

BAABA ADADA:

(Crying)

So much comes into play to turn a noisy home into a quiet one

A home full of laughter turns into that of tears

And then sounds are heard no more

It is a lot that makes a man cry

And it is up to the young man to ask

Where from this transformation? *(He stops)*

BIG BEN:

(Confused) What are you saying old man?

Rubaba Mmahajia Rahma Sabtiu

HASSANA:

I believe it is about his family and him.

BAABA ADADA:

Hassana asked me a question yesterday but I was unable to answer. I want you, Big Ben, to ask me this question; 'Where from this transformation?'

BIG BEN:

I don't understand. Why should I ask you that?

HASSANA:

He says that ask him how he transformed from being a strong young man like you with all his family happy around him to an old lonely man.

BIG BEN:

I am impressed. You really are smart. I didn't really understand him.

BAABA ADADA:

Do not make me a third person. Ask me the question.

BIG BEN:

Ok. Where from this transformation?

BAABA ADADA:

Time is really no one's friend

It is no one's foe either

It is that which causes a succulent skin to suddenly wrinkle

ON THE POLITICAL PODIUM (A STAGE PLAY)

It is that which weakens strong muscles

It is that which causes black hair to suddenly go grey

HASSANA:

But Baaba Adada, does that not make time a foe?

BAABA ADADA:

Of course not, my dear. Hasn't time done enough for us to call him a friend?

BIG BEN:

And what are those things that time has done to merit the name friend? You just stated all the bad things. It made your skin wrinkle, made you weak and turned your hair grey. I don't understand you at all.

BAABA ADADA:

(He smiles) And the same, it will do to you if you are ever blessed with many years. I was once full of life like you. I had all the opportunities to make life better for myself and my people. Wouldn't I at least show gratitude to time for all those times?

BIG BEN:

But hasn't time caused you enough pain to make you recite sorrowful poetry?

HASSANA:

I agree with Big Ben on that?

BAABA ADADA:

Do you actually believe that time is the cause of our pain? Is it not time which offers us the opportunity to overcome the trauma that we go through?

Rubaba Mmahajia Rahma Sabtiu

HASSANA:

(Confused) That's true but ....

BIG BEN:

Who then would you blame for your sorrow?

BAABA ADADA:

(Reciting sorrowfully)

For the greed of one man

So many went through pain

One man, who refused to let peace reign

One man, who wanted it all to himself

Robbing us of our wives and children

Turning our homes into cemeteries

Death, that scar that never heals

Our hearts wounded

Our eyes tired of crying

But today, we have a reason to smile (He ends).

HASSANA:

Hmmm! You have really said a lot.

ON THE POLITICAL PODIUM (A STAGE PLAY)

BIG BEN:

(Confused) Could you say clearly everything that you just recited? My mind is not working straight right now.

BAABA ADADA:

I had a beautiful family. I had a good young lady for a wife and three lovely sons. They were fifteen, ten and three years old respectfully.

HASSANA:

(Smiling) That is a beautiful family indeed.

BAABA ADADA:

(Sadly) I lost them all in the war. All of them.

HASSANA:

(Shocked) My God! Oh Baaba! Accept our condolence.

BAABA ADADA:

Don't worry my dear. Time has healed me.

BIG BEN:

(Confused) You mean your wife and children died in a war?

BAABA ADADA:

Yes, that is what I mean.

BIG BEN:

Which war was that?

Rubaba Mmahajia Rahma Sabtiu

BAABA ADADA:

Did you hear about the war that occurred in the 1970s in this country?

BIG BEN:

No, I don't know about it.

HASSANA:

I learnt about it in my History class.

BIG BEN:

What caused the war?

BAABA ADADA:

All the political parties wanted to be in power and they couldn't afford to see themselves lose the elections. Some loyalists of the parties began fighting amongst themselves until everyone got involved in it and it turned into a war.

HASSANA:

That story scares me.

BIG BEN:

That is very serious. And how come you lost all your family?

BAABA ADADA:

My second son was killed in school when the war just began. My wife and last born died in the hospital and my first born died at the time when we thought the war was almost over. He was playing football with his colleagues. Don't ask me for details because it breaks me down.

ON THE POLITICAL PODIUM (A STAGE PLAY)

BIG BEN:

You have been through a lot indeed.

HASSANA:

Hmmm! You see why you, Big Ben, have absolutely no reason to cause people this much pain? At least you had the opportunity to go to school and you joined gangs who made your life miserable. Your parents didn't help to make things better for you but you can definitely help to make things better for others.

BAABA ADADA:

(He stares at Big Ben) And have you seen a man who has been bitten by a snake before? He jumps for his dear life when he sees even a lizard because the former and the latter have similarities. I live in fear of the fact that so many might go through what we went through. It is an experience I do not want anyone, not even my enemy, to go through.

BIG BEN:

(Sadly) No! No one should go through that at all.

BAABA ADADA:

You have the opportunity now to ensure that the right thing is done. Grab it firmly with all your strength.

HASSANA:

Do something Big Ben.

BIG BEN:

What can I do? I have incited too many people. I have bloated the voters' register. I have bribed people to loot the elections. I have travelled all the regions, towns and villages to give people promises if they vote for Alhaji Yahya. I can't even remember most of these towns and villages.

How do I rectify all that a few hours to the election? And I am not the only opinion leader in this. There are too many of us.

HASSANA:

That is really serious.

BAABA ADADA:

Yet it is never too late. Even if you succeed in convincing just one person to change for the better, you have at least shown a sign of remorse. It is one word of advice that one needs to give to a wise man because that word keeps multiplying in his mind. If you sit here doing nothing, then you will never forgive yourself for whatever will go wrong in this country.

BIG BEN:

Would you two help me to do this? I want to uproot the evil that I have planted as much as possible. Please help me.

HASSANA:

(Happily) I am with you, Big Ben.

BAABA ADADA:

(To the audience) It is by the strength of their number that the ants in the field are able to carry their prey to the nest. *(He turns to Big Ben)* I am with you too Big Ben.

BIG BEN:

Thank you very much. *(To the audience)* However long the moon disappears, someday, it must shine again *(Yaw runs to them)*.

ON THE POLITICAL PODIUM (A STAGE PLAY)

YAW:

(Panting) Hassana! Hassana!

HASSANA:

What is it?

YAW:

(Excited) Greetings to you Baaba Adada.

BAABA ADADA:

Greetings to you Yaw.

YAW:

May you live long in peace and harmony.

HASSANA:

You sound happy.

BAABA ADADA:

He does.

YAW:

I have seen the truth in what you two have been talking about. You wouldn't believe how many people I have succeeded in convincing against those evil plans we made.

HASSANA:

(Happily) Really! That is very wonderful to know.

YAW:

Rubaba Mmahajia Rahma Sabtiu

And I am targeting the members of all the political parties. We must have a free and fair election.

BAABA ADADA:

I am glad. I am very glad.

YAW:

The problem is that so many of them are also opposing me. They can't believe I am going against our hard earned plans. Even my two best friends are against me now and they are threatening to destroy me and anyone who follows me.

BAABA ADADA:

Don't worry. They cannot do anything to you.

YAW:

And seeing Big Ben here, I am wondering whether you could give me the opportunity to convince him even though it might be very hard. He was my boss.

BIG BEN:

(Staring at Yaw sadly) Fortunately, I am already a member of the peace club. I am setting off right now to correct as many of the mistakes I made as possible. And you three should come along with me.

YAW:

(Surprised) That is great. I am really surprised. Baaba Adada and Hassana have some unique ways of convincing people, don't they?

BIG BEN:

They sure do.

ON THE POLITICAL PODIUM (A STAGE PLAY)

HASSANA:

Let's go. Time is running out.

BAABA ADADA:

Where do we start and how far do we go? We need to plan before we act.

BIG BEN:

We will start with the first person we see up until the last person we would see. We would go to every region, every town and every village in this country before the voting begins.

YAW:

That is impossible. It is 11 am already.

BIG BEN:

At least, we would try. I have enough money to take flights in and out of the regions.

HASSANA:

And how do we deal with opposition?

BAABA ADADA:

We would use the best weapon; tolerance.

BIG BEN:

Peace! Peace! Peace!

BAABA ADADA:

Peace!

Rubaba Mmahajia Rahma Sabtiu

HASSANA AND YAW:

(They say in unison) Peace!

BAABA ADADA:

(Happily) God is on our side. For us to be effective, I advise that we move in separate ways.

ALL:

That is true *(They exit in different directions)*.

ON THE POLITICAL PODIUM (A STAGE PLAY)

SCENE TEN:

YAW'S CAMPAIGN

(The sound of drumming is heard in the background and Yaw enters the stage with a drum)

YAW:

(He beats the drum)

Where are you, people of this town?

Where are you, people of this town?

Are you asleep? *(He beats the drum again)*

Wake up and lend me attentive ears

Listen to my every word

Tomorrow we go to the polls *(He beats the drum again)*

Do not vote more than once

Do not argue with your brother or sister who chooses to vote for another party

Do not carry out evil plans that people have incited you to carry

Let whoever wins win *(He beats the drum)*

Remember that our country is all that we have

People of this town, do not cause any kind of trouble in this election

Choose tolerance

Choose peace! *(He beats the drum again)*

Remember every word I say to you

Rubaba Mmahajia Rahma Sabtiu

Do not start an argument on this election with anyone

Do not fight and kill one another for any reason

You are important to this country

Take heed to my words people of this town *(He exits as he talks)*

ON THE POLITICAL PODIUM (A STAGE PLAY)

SCENE ELEVEN:

HASSANA'S CAMPAIGN

(Stage opens with Hassana seated with a document and pen)

HASSANA:

(She writes something and then she turns to the audience) I have written all your concerns and I think that all of them should not and cannot stop us from joining in this last minute peace campaign. As I said earlier, we the women have all that it takes to bring peace into this country. The men are our fathers, brothers, husbands and sons. They are our uncles and grandfathers. Let us try hard to convince them to choose peace because we need it badly *(She removes a small sheet of paper from the document)*. I will read out the last question so that we can all go home and prepare for tomorrow.

THE QUESTION IS:

But Madam Hassana, don't you think that we the women would only make the men furious? Won't our sons turn against us? Won't our brothers see us as betrayers? Won't our husbands divorce us?

Concerned Woman

HASSANA:

(She smiles and talks to the audience) Madam, your question has indeed raised a very critical concern for women in this part of our world especially. But we must know that whenever our fathers, brothers, husbands and sons go wrong, it is up to us to make them see the reality of their actions. If a war occurs right now, it is us the women who will suffer most *(She stands up and begins to pace the stage as she recites)*.

Do we sit down with our hands in our laps?

Do we put our hands to our jaws doing nothing?

Rubaba Mmahajia Rahma Sabtiu

Do we watch helplessly whiles our men commit atrocities?

Can't we convince the women who are with them to stop?

Do we watch our fathers kill themselves?

Do we watch our brothers and husbands live in enmity?

Didn't we bear the burden of carrying our sons in our wombs?

Are we pleased to see the nine months of keeping them safe go astray?

Can we watch our sons and daughters die in front of us?

Think and decide my mothers and sisters.

And remember to make honesty, peace and tolerance your choices *(She comes to pick the document)*. Thank you all very much for your time. I hope you spread the message of peace to everyone who couldn't make it to this gathering. I have to go to another place. Remember to vote for peace *(She exits)*.

ON THE POLITICAL PODIUM (A STAGE PLAY)

SCENE TWELVE:

YAW AND BAABA ADADA MEET

(Baaba Adada enters looking weaker than usual. He sits on the floor as he held his walking stick. He breaths out continuously)

BAABA ADADA:

(Exhausted) Vote for peace my people! Vote for tolerance my people! Let us be honest in this election so that we can enjoy the bliss in our country *(Yaw enters looking tired. He does not see Baaba Adada)*.

YAW:

(He stumbles as he beats the drum) Vote for peace! Vote for peace! *(He also sits on the floor)*.

BAABA ADADA:

(Weakly) We need peace.

YAW:

(Surprised) Baaba Adada. Is this you?

BAABA ADADA:

This is me Yaw. My heart is full of joy.

YAW:

Oh Baaba Adada! Didn't we agree that you should go and rest? It is almost midnight Baaba. Go and have some rest.

BAABA ADADA:

No, Yaw. How can I sleep in this situation? Can't you see that the people themselves are not asleep? They stay awake for tomorrow and we need to convince them to do the right thing.

YAW:

I know. But Big Ben, Hassana and I have enough energy to do this until tomorrow morning. Why don't you let us do that?

BAABA ADADA:

(He laughs) I am a very strong old man remember. Do you know how many people I have convinced to do the right thing? An unbelievable number. Some have even taken it upon themselves to join in the peace campaign.

YAW:

(Smiling) That is great Baaba. I saw a lot of them when I entered the town. They were trying to convince me to do the right thing.

BAABA ADADA:

That is great news. So, where are Hassana and Big Ben?

YAW:

Hassana is travelling from town to town to talk to the women especially and she is succeeding. Big Ben is going to region by region. I don't know which region he is now.

BAABA ADADA:

That is good news. I think we are done with this town. Let us move on to separate towns.

ON THE POLITICAL PODIUM (A STAGE PLAY)

YAW:

But how do you deal with those who oppose you?

BAABA ADADA:

I tell them to at least think about peace before the election. Where they try to be rowdy, I choose tolerance and move away.

YAW:

I think a lot of the opponents are going to do all they can to get back at us. And I am glad that what we are doing is on the televisions and radio stations.

BAABA ADADA:

Yes. That is a good one for us. I saw Big Ben's campaign on television about an hour ago when I was passing by some shops.

YAW:

I just hope that what we are doing would have an impact on tomorrow's election.

BAABA ADADA:

I hope so too. Let's get going then *(They both stand up and begin to walk out)*.

YAW:

(He beats the drum again) Vote for peace my people! Vote for peace my people!

BAABA ADADA:

Remember to be tolerant and honest! Vote for peace! *(They exit)*.

Rubaba Mmahajia Rahma Sabtiu

SCENE THIRTEEN:

BIG BEN'S CAMPAIGN

(Big Ben enters and he sits on the floor)

BIG BEN:

(Looking stressed out) This place is so quiet. Everybody is probably asleep. It is 2:30 am and I haven't even convinced half the people yet. And now there is no one to listen to me anymore *(Continuous thunderstorm is heard in the background)*. It is going to rain and I am in the middle of nowhere. Where are Baaba Adada, Hassana and Yaw? Are they also wondering in this silent darkness for the well-being of their country? Are they trying to repair what I destroyed? *(Crying)* How could I ever forgive myself? *(Reciting sorrowfully)*.

If you put a seed in the soil

You reap a beautiful plant

If you plant evil

Don't expect to always reap goodness

I have ruined my life

But I ruined so many lives as well

In a matter of hours

The result of my evil will show *(He pauses to look in a corner)*

I can see some people over there. But why are they masked? *(Sound of impending danger is heard in the background)*. I am going to talk to them about the peace mission *(He starts approaching the corner and Alhaji Yahya, Adam and Kofi enter from the corner masked)*. Who are you and why are you masked? *(They are quiet)* Won't you talk to me? If you are dressed like

86

this to cause any havoc in this election then please think twice. What do you stand to gain from that? Those party bosses only want to use you to get what they want and then they wouldn't do anything for you after they have gotten what they want. Please brothers or sisters, listen to me.

KOFI:

(He slaps Big Ben) You traitor! How dare you!

BIG BEN:

(He puts his hand to his cheek) Kofi, is this you? My God! Kofi, please don't follow them blindly. You have an opportunity to make it better.

ADAM:

(He laughs loudly) Look at who is talking about making it better. You betrayer!

BIG BEN:

(Surprised) Adam, you too. This is good. At least, we can talk about it. Who is the third person? Is it Dede?

KOFI:

Shut up! If you knew what was coming unto you, you would have worn a metal hat and said your last prayers as well.

BIG BEN:

I wish I could say my last prayers and just forget about everything but I have to clean up the mess I created *(Kofi slaps him again and he falls to the floor)*. Gosh! Why are you slapping me?

KOFI:

I said, 'Shut up!'

Rubaba Mmahajia Rahma Sabtiu

ADAM:

You know what the problem is, Big Ben?

BIG BEN:

What is the problem?

ADAM:

You created a mess that you can never clean.

BIG BEN:

Unless I don't see it, I will surely clean it.

ADAM:

The mess you created is us. You were our master. We obeyed your orders. Today, you have turned against what you taught us to believe in. And we have suddenly taken your place.

KOFI:

That is as true as daylight. The old order changes, yielding place for the new.

BIG BEN:

But Kofi and Adams, doesn't the fact that I, who used to be your master, have changed tell you anything?

KOFI:

It tells us one thing; 'You are a traitor'. You cannot be trusted.

ADAM:

You stabbed Alhaji Yahya in the back upon all that he did for you.

ON THE POLITICAL PODIUM (A STAGE PLAY)

BIG BEN:

What did Alhaji Yahya do for me apart from set me astray against my country? He is the cause of all my problems today.

KOFI:

Watch your words Big Ben, else you would regret it.

BIG BEN:

(He laughs loudly) Be warned that if you urinate in a stream in your town, your relatives are bound to drink from it too. Look at you Kofi, you know very well that you are no match to my strength. Not even ten of you put together so watch your words instead. I am not afraid of anything or anyone.

ADAM:

(Sarcastically) He is sorry Big Ben, the boss. Unfortunately, before he urinated in the stream, you had taught him to disregard his relatives so there is no pain if they drink from the stream. And tell me, Big Ben, what would you do if you met Alhaji Yahya?

BIG BEN:

I am even planning to go and see him and all the other flag bearers of all the political parties to tell them to please reconsider putting the country into danger because it is all that we have.

ADAM:

(Adam and Kofi start clapping as they laugh) That is interesting. Bravo! You definitely are not a much for us.

KOFI:

You sound even more patriotic than those crazy two; Baaba Adada and Hassana.

BIG BEN:

How did you know them?

KOFI:

It is a small world, don't you agree. We do our homework just as you taught us.

ADAM:

They stole our brother, Yaw, from us and they dared to come and talk to us about peace.

BIG BEN:

And why is this third person not talking?

ALHAJI YAHYA:

(Angrily) Because he is too good to let you keep talking.

BIG BEN:

(He stands up in surprise) Alhaji Yahya! It is you.

ALHAJI YAHYA:

Yes, this is me and I got your message very clearly but I wouldn't take it. You should have told me that much earlier before I invested my time, money and trust in you.

BIG BEN:

(He tries to hold Alhaji Yahya but he pushes his hands off him. He went on his knees) Alhaji Yahya, please try to understand. Please make the country peaceful.

ALHAJI YAHYA:

Kofi!

ON THE POLITICAL PODIUM (A STAGE PLAY)

KOFI:

Yes, Alhaji.

ALHAJI YAHYA:

Adam!

ADAM:

Yes, Sir.

ALHAJI YAHYA:

I have had enough of him. Let's get out of here. *(He stares at Big Ben)* A pad that breaks a pot of water must not remain on the head. Good bye Big Ben. Go and preach peace somewhere else *(He takes out a gun and shoots at Big Ben who screams in pain).*

BIG BEN:

(Screaming in pain) My God! Please consider the country.

KOFI:

(He laughs loudly) See the end of Big Ben, the patriotic citizen. How pathetic!

BIG BEN:

(He stares at Kofi in pain) When a dying man cries, it is not because of where he is going which he knows nothing about but it is because of what he wishes he would have done in the world he is leaving. The people alive around him must learn lessons from his pain if they are wise.

ALHAJI YAHYA:

(Angrily) Stop all that nonsense.

BIG BEN:

(Crying) Dead though the oil palm may be, the maggot in it lives on.

ALHAJI YAHYA:

(He fires at him for the second time and Big Ben screams even louder) See you in Hell.

BIG BEN:

Oh my God! He has killed me *(He fell to the ground dead).*

ALHAJI YAHYA:

(He angrily hits him with his leg) You son of a bitch! You didn't know whom you were dealing with, did you?

KOFI:

Too bad for him. The very strong Big Ben is finally dead. We will teach the others a lesson.

ALHAJI YAHYA:

(He points to Kofi and Adam) And you two should be very careful with me as well. Pretend you didn't see any of this happen.

ADAM:

(Overcome by fear) I didn't know you were going to kill him. I thought you were just supposed to scare him.

ALHAJI YAHYA:

(Annoyed, he points the gun at Adam) Do you want to follow him?

ADAM:

ON THE POLITICAL PODIUM (A STAGE PLAY)

(Scared) No! No! No!

ALHAJI YAHYA:

Let's go then *(They exit).*

Rubaba Mmahajia Rahma Sabtiu

SCENE FOURTEEN:

YAW AND HASSANA MEET

(Stage opens with Yaw standing in the centre of the stage)

YAW:

Peace feels like honey trickling down the throat. You will never know how it tastes until you try it. Hmmm! Thank God I am safe after everything *(He pauses)*. But why is Hassana taking such a long time? *(Hassana enters)*.

HASSANA:

I am here now. Safe and sound by God's grace.

YAW:

Good. I thought something bad might have happened to you.

HASSANA:

Surprisingly, I am very ok. I heard you had an attack yesterday night.

YAW:

Yes. Baaba Adada told you, right?

HASSANA:

Yes, he did. I went to his house this morning before going to vote.

YAW:

So, how was the environment of your polling station like?

ON THE POLITICAL PODIUM (A STAGE PLAY)

HASSANA:

Very peaceful. So far, nobody has tried anything funny.

YAW:

I hope it remains like that till the election is over.

HASSANA:

But I am worried, tell me the details of the attack because Baaba Adada refused to tell me.

YAW:

I was attacked by Kofi and Adam.

HASSANA:

(Surprised) Your own friends?

YAW:

Our friendship ended the day I chose to go with peace. Anyway, I was smarter than them so in the end, they had to run away for their lives.

HASSANA:

Thank God!

YAW:

I went to check to see if Baaba Adada was ok because I knew they know his house and they might try to attack him as well but they didn't come there.

HASSANA:

That is good. I hope they join the peace campaign after the election.

Rubaba Mmahajia Rahma Sabtiu

YAW:

I doubt those two would ever want peace. I feel that something would go wrong. My intuition hardly makes a mistake.

HASSANA:

Hmmm! Let's just pray and hope for the best. But have you heard from Big Ben?

YAW:

I haven't seen nor heard from him.

HASSANA:

Me too. Baaba Adada too has not heard from him. I hope he is ok.

YAW:

I know his attack would be more dangerous than mine but he is a very strong man so I am hoping no one can do anything to him. I hope he returns to us safely.

HASSANA:

I hope so too.

YAW:

Let's go and check on Baaba Adada then. That old man amazes me. I admire his patriotism.

HASSANA:

He is such an inspiration.

ON THE POLITICAL PODIUM (A STAGE PLAY)

YAW:

I wonder why I didn't meet such people earlier in my life. I guess I would have been a much better person than the horrible one I was some few days earlier.

HASSANA:

There is a reason for everything. At least, be glad that you didn't end up in that kind of lifestyle.

YAW:

I am very glad and I am going to try my very best to let Kofi and Adam see the need to enjoy the peace and calm I feel in my heart especially.

HASSANA:

I wish you all the best *(Continuous thunderstorm is heard in the background)*. Let's hurry up. It looks like it might rain.

YAW:

I hope it rains after the elections instead if not there would be trouble *(They rush out)*.

SCENE FIFTEEN:

(Sound of a dirge is heard in the background as Baaba Adada, Hassana and Yaw sit sorrowfully)

YAW:

(Crying) Why? Why? Why?

HASSANA:

(Crying) Calm down Yaw. The harm has already been done. God knows best why He does what He does.

YAW:

But how can I ever forgive myself?

HASSANA:

You tried your best to correct all the wrongs. That is praiseworthy.

YAW:

But haven't I contributed to so many losing their lives?

BAABA ADADA:

(Sadly) Hmmm! Yaw, calm down. Today, you are a hero. Big Ben is a hero too. That is enough to call him a good person.

HASSANA:

Alhaji Yahya is so wicked and heartless. How could he stoop this low?

YAW:

I want to turn myself in to the police.

ON THE POLITICAL PODIUM (A STAGE PLAY)

HASSANA:

No Yaw! You cannot do that.

YAW:

I can't live with the guilt Hassana. I can never live with it.

BAABA ADADA:

A man must face the consequences of what he does. You will serve as a role model to the youth when you do.

HASSANA:

We are in the media as saviours of this country. The people can't bear to see you in prison, Yaw. Turn yourself in. It will be another peace strategy. Besides, you didn't commit any crime. You will only help the police to understand issues better.

YAW:

(Crying) Where would I have gone to if this country had gone to war? If you see a neighbour's beard on fire, you put water to yours. Haven't I seen all the countries that are so insecure around me?

HASSANA:

(To the audience) It is exactly a week after the election. A few people have been killed. Few houses have been burnt. Few ballot boxes were stolen. Big Ben's body was found. Adam had confessed all the evil they had done. He could not stand the torture of his guilt. All the bad politicians and their accomplices will face the law. But now, everything is calm and peace reigns! *(Lights go out on stage)*

SCENE SIXTEEN:

IN BAABA ADADA'S HOUSE

(Baaba Adada snores in his sleep and is dressed as in the first scene)

HASSANA:

Ei! Why is Papa sleeping for so long today? *(Tapping him)* Papa, please wake up. Lunch is ready.

BAABA ADADA:

(Snoring) Oooo! Peace reigns! Peace reigns!

HASSANA:

Papa, please wake up else your food would be cold *(Adam enters)*.

ADAM:

Why are you waking him up, Hassana? Don't you know that he could get a headache?

HASSANA:

Brother Adam, daddy has been sleeping since he came from the hospital and he hasn't eaten anything yet. His lunch time is almost over and the doctor advised that he should not skip his lunch. And he is also saying some funny things in his sleep.

ADAM:

And what is he saying?

BAABA ADADA:

(Still snoring) Peace reigns! Peace reigns! Peace reigns!

ON THE POLITICAL PODIUM (A STAGE PLAY)

ADAMS:

(He laughs) Daddy and his peace talks! He has even sent it to his sleep *(Shaking Baaba Adada)* Papa! Papaa!

BAABA ADADA:

(He wakes up annoyed) What is it? Can't you see… *(He stares at them in surprise)*.

ADAM:

(Smiling) It is time for your lunch Papa. Remember the doctor's advice?

HASSANA:

(Worried) And your food is getting cold.

BAABA ADADA:

(He kept staring at them) But Hassana and Adam, you were…

ADAM:

(Worried) We were what?

BAABA ADADA:

(He laughs loudly as he stands up) This is incredible! The election is rather tomorrow.

ADAM AND HASSANA:

(Confused) What?

BAABA ADADA:

(He smiles happily) It was all a dream. May it never come to pass. Peace reigns!

THE END!!!